CYRUS EATON

Champion *for* Peace

Story & Art by
Richard Rudnicki

NIMBUS
PUBLISHING

Nimbus Publishing Limited
3731 Mackintosh St, Halifax, NS B3K 5A5
(902) 455-4286 nimbus.ca

Printed and bound in China

NB1182

Cover illustration: Richard Rudnicki
Cover design: Heather Bryan
Interior design: Jenn Embree

Library and Archives Canada Cataloguing in Publication

Rudnicki, Richard, author
Cyrus Eaton : champion of peace / Richard Rudnicki.
Issued in print and electronic formats.
ISBN 978-1-77108-396-6 (bound).—ISBN 978-1-77108-397-3 (pdf)

1. Eaton, Cyrus Stephen, 1883-1979—Juvenile literature. 2. Industrialists—United States--Biography—Juvenile literature. 3. Industrialists—Canada—Biography--Juvenile literature. 4. Pacifists—United States—Biography—Juvenile literature. 5. Pacifists—Canada—Biography—Juvenile literature. 6. Nobel Prize winners—United States—Biography--Juvenile literature. 7. Nobel Prize winners—Canada—Biography—Juvenile literature. 8. Pugwash (N.S.)—Biography—Juvenile literature. I. Title.

CT275.E242R84 2016   C813'.6   C2015-907610-2
                                          C2015-907611-0

Canada Council   Conseil des arts
for the Arts   du Canada

Nimbus Publishing acknowledges the financial support for its publishing activities from the Government of Canada through the Canada Book Fund (CBF) and the Canada Council for the Arts, and from the Province of Nova Scotia. We are pleased to work in partnership with the Province of Nova Scotia to develop and promote our creative industries for the benefit of all Nova Scotians.

"We showed that people of different languages and philosophies can get together to discuss important questions, come to common understanding, and part great friends.

–CYRUS EATON

CYRUS EATON was six years old during the great fire of 1890. There'd been other fires in Pugwash, Nova Scotia, but this one threatened his family home.

With shouts of encouragement, his family, their neighbours, and friends attacked the flames with shovels, axes, and sticks. They pulled sheds out of the way. They soaked blankets in water to wet the ground. Everyone worked together to save the neighbourhood.

The Eatons owned a farm, a general store, and a post office in
the small coastal village of Pugwash. Every day, young Cyrus,
like everyone in his family, had jobs to do. On the farm, he
herded cows down to the river and helped milk them. When
he was four years old, Cyrus began driving a horse-drawn
wagon to the mill to have grain ground for the farm animals.
Often he would even take care of the family's store by
himself. His father said he was smart and could be trusted.

Cyrus was curious about everything. He loved to learn, and read every book he could get his hands on. Books fed his imagination and hunger for new ideas. He also enjoyed going to plays at the theatre, reading poetry, and found inspiration in philosophy and reading the Bible.

When he got older, Cyrus studied religion, philosophy, and business at college. His marks were high, and he was good at debating and sports. He began asking big questions like, "How can I make a difference?" and "Is there any way to make the world a better place?"

The more Cyrus read and talked with others, the more ideas he was able to consider. He thought he might become a minister, like his Uncle Charles.

Cyrus's uncle, Reverend Charles Eaton, was a friend of **John D. Rockefeller Senior**, the head of a business empire in the United States. Rockefeller was a generous man who gave to many good causes. When he met Cyrus, he liked him right away and offered him a summer job. Cyrus proved himself and soon moved to Cleveland, Ohio, to work for Mr. Rockefeller, running errands and carrying golf bags.

Rockefeller became interested in a business in western Canada that had been formed to buy electric power companies. He sent Cyrus to investigate, but by the time he got there, the business had fallen apart. Instead of being upset, Cyrus saw a good opportunity and borrowed money to buy the power companies himself.

Cyrus then decided to buy other companies, combining them to make them bigger and more profitable. He quickly became very successful: everything he touched seemed to turn to gold!

In 1914, when he was thirty years old with a young family, Cyrus Eaton became a millionaire. Still, his ambitions continued to grow. He formed the United Light & Power Company, which **generated** and sold electricity, and by 1929, the company was worth billions.

*For definitions of all the words in bold, see the glossary at the back of the book.

That same year, the financial markets in the United States suddenly collapsed and companies everywhere went out of business. It was the beginning of a decade of poverty known today as the **Great Depression.**

There weren't enough jobs. People had no money and went hungry. Cyrus Eaton's businesses began to fail, and he lost almost everything. One Christmas during those years, all he had to bring to his daughter's house was fruit and a ten-dollar bill.

It took almost ten years before the Great Depression finally ended, and Cyrus Eaton was eager to rebuild his fortune. Since he knew about the generation of electric power, that's where he started.

Cyrus and his businesses became successful again, and after a few years he made enough money to buy a large lake in northwestern Ontario. He knew there were **iron ore** deposits beneath the lake and if he could reach the minerals he could sell them to companies making weapons and equipment for the war. He took a risk and drained the lake. It cost eight million dollars. Then he sold the iron ore and made a fortune.

For the next twenty years, Cyrus Eaton purchased, sold, and traded businesses, and built an empire even bigger than before.

By the time he reached his forties, Cyrus had learned a lot, and had ideas he wanted to share. He began to write letters to leaders in business and politics. He wondered why wealthy business owners did not treat their workers more fairly. Cyrus believed that it would be better for businesses if people helped run the companies they worked for. "Workers who are treated with dignity," he said, "will put their hearts in the business." Because of his powerful position in society, Cyrus's essays, articles, and editorials were published and read widely.

At this time in his life, Cyrus lived in Cleveland, Ohio, but kept a close connection to his home village of Pugwash. Throughout his business career, he enjoyed nature. He bought land with woods, old farms, and lakes in Deep Cove near Blandford, Nova Scotia, and turned it into a wildlife sanctuary and summer home for his family.

Cyrus was very much part of his home community. When another fire destroyed the downtown of Pugwash a few years earlier, he had helped rebuild it. He was convinced that education was the key to a better world, and he had a modern high school built in the village. He also gave generously to many colleges, including Acadia University in Wolfville, Nova Scotia.

In 1939 tragedy struck again. The leaders of the world failed to resolve deep differences between their countries and the Second World War began. It didn't end until 1945, when the United States dropped an **atomic bomb** on Japan, killing hundreds of thousands of people.

The world was horrified by the bomb's destructive power. Along with many others, Cyrus Eaton wanted to find a way to stop the use of **nuclear weapons** like the atomic bomb. He believed there had to be a better way to solve problems between countries.

Even though Cyrus made money in rubber, steel, electricity, and finance, he thought of himself as a farmer. He raised cattle and geese, and took great joy in being close to the land. The world seemed like a big farm to him, and all its people were one big family. He thought if families can work through disagreements, countries can too.

He wanted leaders around the world in politics, business, and science to come together to find a way for their countries to get along. He was not yet sure how.

In time, Cyrus had thirteen grandchildren. Every summer they came without their parents to join him and his wife, Anne, at their farm in Deep Cove. There they swam, canoed, played sports, and learned about farming and fishing. They learned to love nature and the outdoors.

Cyrus enjoyed taking his grandchildren on picnics and having dinners with them. He asked them challenging questions, and listened closely to their answers. He knew it was only a matter of time before today's children become tomorrow's world leaders.

One day after lunch, Cyrus's grandchildren gathered to play a game of croquet. Two of the older players, who could shoot straighter and farther, began taking advantage of the younger ones and winning. Sharp words were said, and feelings were hurt. The argument grew ugly. Just then, a few of the grandchildren who had been hanging back stepped forward.

"Stop fighting!" one of them urged.

"What would happen if we started the game over, and made the teams fair this time?" another asked. They all agreed.

Anne watched how the children resolved the unfair competition and she told her husband. She and Cyrus thought it would be wonderful if countries could work things out just like that too—by talking instead of trying to overpower each other.

Cyrus had an idea. In 1955, he began inviting people to gatherings at his homes in Canada and the United States to ask questions, share ideas, and explore ways to understand and try to fix the world's problems. He encouraged these people to share different points of view and learn to compromise. He helped put them at ease by inviting them on picnics and playing sports with them, just like he'd done with his grandchildren.

In 1957, concern was growing around the world. A call went out from famous philosophers and scientists to discuss the dangers of nuclear weapons. Recalling the gatherings at his homes and how well they had gone, Cyrus believed if countries worked together, peace could be achieved.

Even though not everyone agreed with Cyrus, he offered to host a four-day meeting. Some open-minded thinkers accepted, and powerful scientists from around the world— the United States, China, Russia, Great Britain, France, and other countries—gathered in Pugwash, Nova Scotia.

Cyrus insisted they get to know each other as human beings. So they played croquet, had picnics, hiked, and took boat rides together. The relaxing time helped the scientists bond and really listen to each other as they thought about how to eliminate nuclear weapons from the world.

Ever since then, Cyrus Eaton's seven-bedroom home overlooking Northumberland Strait has been known as Thinkers Lodge. The conference in Pugwash was so successful that Cyrus offered to hold another one the following year, this time in Quebec.

Cyrus was thrilled when the third conference, held in Austria in 1958 and sponsored by the Austrian government, drew eighty scientists from twenty-two nations. When they met, there was an audience of fifteen thousand, including the president of Austria.

Over the next six years, thinkers from around the world met ten times, including twice in Pugwash. Scientists, scholars, and public figures came together to discuss **nuclear energy** and weapons, and other important issues. They declared that countries must stop building up nuclear **arsenals** and threatening to use them.

By 1963 the peace conferences started at Thinkers Lodge had the world's attention, and the world's major powers—the United States, the United Kingdom, and the **USSR**—signed a treaty banning nuclear testing. It wasn't a complete ban, but it was a good start.

More peace conferences followed. There have been over sixty to date. Known as the "Pugwash Conferences on Science and World Affairs," or the "Pugwash Movement" for short, they are held in cities around the world—sometimes in Pugwash. At the meetings, hundreds of scientists, members of government, and international leaders explore creative ways to solve the world's most difficult problems.

Cyrus never dreamed in 1957 that the first meeting at
Thinkers Lodge would lead to an international movement
that still exists today.

In 1995 the same conferences that started at Thinkers Lodge won the **Nobel Peace Prize**, along with noted Polish-born British physicist **Joseph Rotblat**, one of the conference's founders. They were rewarded "for their efforts to diminish the part played by nuclear weapons in international politics and, in the longer run, to eliminate such weapons."

There is still much conflict in the world, but Cyrus Eaton and the others who shared solutions to tough problems at Thinkers Lodge helped make our world safer and more peaceful for all.

CYRUS EATON TIMELINE

1883   Born in Pugwash, Nova Scotia.

1899   Graduates from Amherst Academy in Nova Scotia and begins studies at Woodstock College in Ontario.

1901   While visiting his uncle Reverend Charles Eaton in Cleveland, Ohio, Cyrus meets John D. Rockefeller Sr. He is introduced to the world of finance.

1905   Graduates from McMaster University with a Bachelor of Arts degree and a major in philosophy. Moves to Cleveland to work for the East Ohio Gas Company, a company associated with John D. Rockefeller Sr.

1907   Marries Margaret House. Establishes his own business developing gas companies. Takes a loan and buys other similar companies in western Canada. Later, he combines them into the Canada Gas & Electric Corporation. He continues this trend in Iowa, Kansas, and Nebraska.

1912   Sets up Continental Gas & Electric. Buys a house outside Cleveland, Ohio, named Acadia Farms. Begins raising his seven children.

1913   Becomes a citizen of the United States.

1914   Outbreak of the First World War. Cyrus becomes a millionaire.

1916 Buys a substantial interest in Otis & Company, an investment banking and stockbroking company in Cleveland. The company's partners have assets of more than $200 million.

1918 End of the First World War.

1919 Cyrus begins combining all of the independent phone companies in Ohio under a single company, Ohio State Telephone. He then combines this company with Ohio Bell.

1920 Over the next ten years, Cyrus quickly acquires a large empire of successful businesses in investment, utility, steel, and rubber. He becomes a director in dozens of wealthy companies, and invests money in the United States steel industry. He founds a museum, and is generous to communities.

1929 The Wall Street stock market crashes, and the Great Depression begins. Downtown Pugwash is destroyed by flood and fire. Cyrus donates money to rebuild the village. Over the next several years, he loses most of his wealth because of the Depression.

1931 Acquires a three-thousand-acre summer estate in Upper Blandford, Nova Scotia, named Deep Cove Farm.

1932 Supports the presidential nomination of Franklin D. Roosevelt.

1934 Divorces from his first wife, Margaret House.

1936 As the world begins to recover from the Great Depression, Cyrus begins rebuilding his fortune.

1938 President Roosevelt asks Cyrus to help develop the St. Lawrence Seaway.

1939 Beginning of the Second World War.

1942 Acquires Steep Rock Lake in northwestern Ontario. Drains the lake to yield iron ore at the rate of a million tons a year.

1943 Becomes director of the Chesapeake and Ohio Railway.

1945 Atomic bombing of Hiroshima and Nagasaki, Japan. End of the Second World War.

1948 Supports Harry S. Truman's presidential campaign.

1951 Raises prize-winning Scotch Shorthorn cattle and begins holding cattle auctions twice a year at Acadia Farms in Ohio.

1953 Becomes board chairman of the Kentucky Coal Co.

1954 Turns his family home in Pugwash into a permanent site for conferences, workshops, and educational events. Appointed chairman of the Chesapeake & Ohio Railway.

1955 Offers to sponsor the conference called for in the Russell-Einstein Manifesto. Sends one of his Scotch Shorthorn cattle to the Soviet Union to help improve Russian beef.

1957 At the height of the Cold War, Cyrus sponsors and hosts the first of the Pugwash Conferences on Science and World Affairs, with twenty-two distinguished scientists from ten nations. Marries his second wife, Anne Kinder Jones.

1958 The Pugwash Peace Conference, held in Austria, draws an audience of fifteen thousand, with eighty scientists from twenty-two nations who condemn nuclear weapons. Cyrus makes his first trip to the Soviet Union.

1960 Invested with the Lenin Peace Prize for his efforts at a harmonious relationship with the Soviet Union. Calls on President of Cuba, Fidel Castro, in New York for a UN meeting, to pay his respects.

1962 Ranked eighth in a list of the ten most controversial Americans.

1963 Celebrates the signing of the Nuclear Test Ban Treaty.

1967 Named Man of the Year by the Cleveland Press Club.

1969 Attempts to intervene and diplomatically end the Vietnam War.

1979 Dies at Acadia Farms near Cleveland, Ohio. Buried at Deep Cove Farm in Nova Scotia.

GLOSSARY

Arsenal
A collection (or collections) of military equipment and weapons.

Atomic bomb
A nuclear weapon that uses a nuclear reaction to split atoms to release vast, destructive energy from a small amount of matter. Considered a weapon of mass destruction, the atomic bomb was used twice in warfare by the United States against Japan near the end of the Second World War, resulting in the deaths of about two hundred thousand people.

Finance
The management of money, often by large companies or governments.

Generation (of electricity)
The process of creating electric power from some form of physical or chemical resource found in nature.

Great Depression (1929–1939)
A sharp downturn in the economies of the world that originated in the United States after the fall of the stock market in 1929. International business dropped by 50 percent and unemployment in some countries was as high as 33 percent. Construction, farming, mining, and logging were deeply affected.

Iron ore
Minerals or rocks from which iron can be taken to make steel.

Nobel Prize
Five highly respected monetary prizes established by Alfred Nobel and awarded annually for Peace, Chemistry, Physics, Medicine,

and Literature. The 1995 Peace prize was awarded equally to the Pugwash Conferences on Science and World Affairs and Joseph Rotblat, a founder.

Nuclear energy
The power released by a reaction using fuel made from uranium to make weapons of mass destruction, or to generate electricity.

Nuclear weapon
A dangerous device, like a bomb, that uses the explosive power of nuclear energy.

Rockefeller Sr., John D. (1839–1937)
A wealthy American businessperson who supported many good causes. He was a co-founder of the Standard Oil Company, a leader in the oil industry.

Rotblat, Joseph (1908–2005)
A Polish physicist, he was the only one to leave the team of physicists building the atomic bomb for the US in the Second World War because of his strong opposition to nuclear weapons. The work he did helped lead to the 1963 Partial Nuclear Test Ban Treaty. He signed on to the 1955 Russell–Einstein Manifesto calling for nuclear disarmament with eleven other prominent nuclear physicists and intellectuals, including Albert Einstein. Rotblat was one of the founders of the Pugwash Peace Conferences.

USSR
Abbreviation for Union of Soviet Socialist Republics, and known as the Soviet Union. It was formed in 1922 and eventually included Russia, Ukraine, and thirteen other communist republics where property and resources were owned in common and not by individuals. It dissolved in 1991.

SELECTED BIBLIOGRAPHY

Books and articles

Eaton, Cyrus. "A Capitalist Looks at Labour." *University of Chicago Law Review*, 14.3, April 1947, 332–336.

Gleisser, Marcus. *The World of Cyrus Eaton*, New York: A. S. Barnes and Co., 1965.

Gibson, M. Allen. *Beautiful Upon the Mountains: A Portrait of Cyrus Eaton*. Lancelot Press, 1977.

Archives

McMaster University Archives and Reading Collections: Cyrus Eaton Collection

Western Reserve Historical Society: Eaton papers

Websites

Thinkers Lodge in Pugwash, Nova Scotia: thinkerslodge.org

The Cyrus Eaton Foundation: deepcove.org

Thinkers Lodge Oral Histories: thinkerslodgeoralhistories.com

Pugwash Conferences on Science and World Affairs: pugwash.org

Canadian Pugwash Group: pugwashgroup.ca

Village of Pugwash, Nova Scotia: pugwashvillage.com